The Holly King & The Oak King
A Pagan Children's Tale

J. C. Artemisia

Illustrated by Sarah A. Chase

Copyright © 2019 J. C. Artemisia

All rights reserved.

ISBN-10: 1099650437
ISBN-13: 978-1099650437

DEDICATION

To my children, may you grow in patience and balance, and may you always have faith in change. And an extra special thanks to Trystan, who inspired me with his prayer to "the king of dreams."

ACKNOWLEDGMENTS

As with all myths and lore, the details of this story have changed from one telling to the next. Some people say The Holly & Oak Kings are two aspects of the same being; some say their battles occur on the equinoxes rather than on the solstices. There are many tales about these two kings, and all are important if they bring joy and goodness to people's lives. This is one such story, and I hope you enjoy it.

After the tale you will find a poem for each king and activities for solstice celebration.

Blessed be,
J. C. Artemisia

Long ago, there was a mountain so tall it scraped the sky, reaching the spirits of the sun, the moon, and the stars. The spirits admired this mountain and blessed its forest with an abundance of magick, allowing it to be both warm and cool, dark and light at once.

One night, when the mountain lay in half-summer half-winter slumber, a rumble climbed through the tall peaks, rattling trees, crumbling rocks, and shivering out into the universe. The echoes from this quake crashed into two nearby stars, knocking them loose from the sky.

One of the fallen stars nestled into a patch of holly; the other tumbled onto oak tree roots. When the stars finally flickered out, the forest creatures bowed their heads. The weather reflected their sadness with soft rain and deep wind, lifting the crumbled stars, swirling and pulsing with the mountain's magick. Twin gods, the Holly and Oak Kings, were born from this stardust.

Oak and Holly settled into the forest, aligning with the shifts in mountain temperament and weather. Oak was playful and spirited, always adventuring with his chirpy robin friend. Oak's energy buzzed through the forest—lighting the sky, lifting the air, and waking the flowers on the eastern mountain side.

Holly dwelled on the western slope with his team of eight, white stags. Holly was quieter and more reflective than his brother. He foraged and prepared, preferring stillness and darkness for reverent thought and dreaming. But for all his concentration, he was also strong and steadfast—always caring for the night creatures around him.

Despite their differences, the brothers loved each other. They prayed daily at a stone table on the mountain's north side, frequently walking together afterward, but most often, dueling— the kings lived to battle one another.

One afternoon, while walking an eastern trail, the brothers admired colorful gardens blooming in the sunshine. Fiery tiger lilies stretched on strong stalks, but beneath the peppered orange petals, soft white buds shied away. "Moonflowers," said Holly. "Look how they hide. The sunlight on this mountainside is too bright; they will not survive." Holly raised his vine-wrapped walking staff toward the sky and magickally pulled the leafy forest canopy closed like a curtain. As darkness covered the forest path, the moonflowers yawned open their delicate petals. The Holly King smiled at the sleepy flowers, but his brother wasn't so happy.

"Brother!" the Oak King bellowed, "the moonflowers are not hiding—they are *protected*. With time, the tiger lilies will grow larger to cast greater shade, but they cannot thrive in shadows." Oak raised his twisted, honey-gold staff and reopened the forest canopy.

Holly aimed his staff once more, but before he could cast his power at the treetops, Oak swung his staff to meet Holly's—*CRACK!* Oak thrusted forward; Holly parried and charged. The Oak King's staff glowed with powerful orange-heat, while Holly's staff frosted over with silvery-blue magick. The kings battled, and their energy grew, but before either could claim victory, the ground began to rumble. Both brothers yielded to the familiar tremor—a deep, echoing quake like the one that had borne them from the skies.

"Are you okay?" Holly asked when the quake stopped.

"Yes," Oak replied, "but listen." The mountain was consumed in silence and stillness.

The kings hurried back down the forest path to find the great stone table cracked in half. Beneath it, a fault line zig-zagged down the mountain face. "We must follow this trail," Oak said. Holly agreed, and the brothers set on their quest.

The fault line led the brothers to the base of their mountain. "This is the land of humans," Holly assessed. "Our exploring must end here; we are not of this world."

"That may be so," Oak replied, "but we share this earth's plane. Something is wrong with our Earth Mother; I can feel it."

"I feel it, too," said Holly, "but our forms may frighten the humans for they are mortal, and we are of the stars." He stamped his staff on the ground. Glittering smoke swirled around him, and when it cleared, he had transformed into a white stag. Oak too, struck the ground with his staff, transforming into a robin. In these forms, the kings journeyed off their mountain.

In the human world, the kings observed a land that could not alter its climate as their magickal mountain could. Humans everywhere scrambled to sew and harvest crops under unpredictable weather. The Oak King robin flew over farm lands that had flooded after too much rain. The Holly King stag wandered in forests behind houses, listening to parents singing wishes and lullaby-promises to their children.

Seeing this distress, the kings returned to their mountain, resumed their natural forms, and prayed. The spirits echoed in response, "What do the humans need to thrive and to care for the earth?"

Oak answered first, "They require more sunlight to dry the land and return to work."

Holly disagreed, "These people are tired. They need darkness and rest to heal."

Thunder boomed, and aurora colors splashed across the skies. The universe called, "Twin brothers, from your mountain overlooking the human realm, you will observe the needs of the people below and determine a new path for the sun's warmth and light."

The kings argued more feverishly than ever with empathy and compassion for their earthly siblings. They drew their staffs, ready to duel and trust the victor to the universe.

Passionate swings cut through the mountain air, each brother fighting for the path he thought was best. In the end, Holly struck the final blow, thwarting his brother so keenly that Oak was cast far into the distant stars.

For one whole year, the Holly King navigated low, even paths for the sun. In the human world, days were short and cool, and nights were long and quiet. People lit candles and decorated trees with colorful seed-balls to feed wintering animals. Though the weather was cold, the atmosphere was festive and warm. Holly smiled to create such peace. Beneath the decked trees, he hid small trinkets and treats for children to find and enjoy.

But soon, the plants withered, and people became listless with little daylight for work and play. When the Oak King returned, the earth had become weak and fragile. "Brother, it is time to end your reign," Oak demanded, drawing his staff. "The earth cannot grow in such darkness."

Holly replied, "Brother, you would rather scorch its soil with sunlight!" He battled to defend his rule, but he was tired from carrying the weight of the sun. Oak quickly gained favor, and with a crushing blow from his glowing staff, he cast his brother far into the stars.

Another year turned, this time with the Oak King raising the sun's power high to the magickal mountain's peak. Slowly, the land thawed, and people emerged from their homes like flowers from their buds. They danced and sang, lighting fires to honor the returned warmth. Oak was happy, and he blessed the land with vibrant colors and lush vegetation.

But after some time, the humans wilted, the ground dried, and the crops crumbled. When the Holly King returned, he looked upon the parched earth and cried, "Brother, please hear me! I love you as I love our Mother Earth, and that is why I must insist you let me lay the heavy sun to rest."

"Brother, I cannot let you freeze the earth into another year-long sleep!" Oak replied, preparing to fight.

The brothers dueled through the forest. The Oak King, tired and sore, took a knee in defeat when they reached the great stone table. He observed the deep fracture splitting the stone's surface. "You win, today," Oak sighed. "But I will return in just a half-year's time to challenge your strength and intentions."

Holly helped his brother to his feet. "I will be here," he promised.

From that day on, the solstices were marked deeply with battles twice per year on the magickal mountain. The Holly King charts the sunlight low to cool the earth, and then his brother returns at Yule, strong and rested to lift the sun high. The kings fight honorably with full resolve each solstice, trusting the strength of their intentions to the universe, and blessing the earth with a balance of light and life.

To Slowly Fading Sun, We Bid Goodbye

To slowly fading sun, we bid goodbye,
preparing now for earth to take its rest;
the Holly King will calm the tired sky.

His brother, Oak, had perched the fires high,
our daylight hours stretching from their crest.
To slowly fading sun, we bid goodbye.

The kings engaged in battle and did vie
to win the throne for he whose path was best.
The Holly King will calm the tired sky.

All Oak's advances, Holly did defy,
prevailing in his winter-focused quest.
To slowly fading sun, we bid goodbye.

Soon, nature's palette he will simplify—
though stark, the harvest colors mean we're blessed.
The Holly King will calm the tired sky.

He'll care for us as winter freeze draws nigh,
warming our long-night dreams with joyful jest.
To slowly fading sun, we bid goodbye;
the Holly King will calm the tired sky.

Light Will Return Again When Morning Comes

Light will return again when morning comes.
Though recent days have grown so dark and gray,
the Oak King's might will soon restore the sun.

After the solstice battle he had won,
he sent his brother, Holly, far away.
Light will return again when morning comes.

Cold weather has now only just begun,
but light grows brighter with each passing day.
The Oak King's might will soon restore the sun.

And winter's icy grip will be undone
as springing buds and colors soon give way.
Light will return again when morning comes.

Upon sweet sands and soils we will run,
then sit in gardens where we work and play.
The Oak King's might will soon restore the sun.

Around the fires we all dance as one;
a song of thanks, to man in green we pray.
Light will return again when morning comes;
the Oak King's might will soon restore the sun.

Winter Solstice Activity: Growing Warmth and Light

The Winter Solstice is the darkest day of the year. The sun rises late and sets early. But on this solstice, the Oak King will win the battle against his brother. Over the next six months, the Oak King will make the sun stronger and brighter, and the days will grow longer.

During this season, it is good to work on personal energy. As the sun grows warmer and brighter, you can practice sending positive light into the world, too. This can be as simple as connecting with kindness to yourself and to others.

A Memory of Kindness: Write or draw an example of a kindness someone else did for you. How did this make you feel?

Kind to Self: It is important to be kind and patient with yourself as you grow and learn new things. Write or draw an example of a time you were kind or patient with yourself.

Sharing Acts of Kindness: For some families, a common Yule-time practice includes giving gifts. Kindness can be a wonderful gift to share with others. Some examples of simple kindnesses include sharing a smile, lending a helping hand, and praying for blessings. In the space below, write or draw about some kindnesses you could share with the people in your life.

Summer Solstice Activity: My Power Meditation and Goal Setting

The Summer Solstice marks the longest, brightest day of the year. The Oak King has worked hard to lift the sun high into the sky. Now, the Holly King will triumph and take over, leading the sun back down until Yule. Take some time to feel the summer sun on your skin—take in its warmth and power; these are blessings for you—how will you use them?

My Power Meditation: Plant yourself firmly on the earth. Stretch your arms and fingers high toward the summer sun. Accept its warmth and feel yourself growing tall and strong like a tree. What are some of your greatest strengths? Are you a great artist or sports player? Are you kind? Are you funny? Write or draw some of your strengths—your powers—here.

Goal Setting: Think about some things you would like to learn or experience. What challenges might you face, and who/what will help you when you need support? Write or draw about them here.

Read More Pagan Children's Books
By J. C. Artemisia

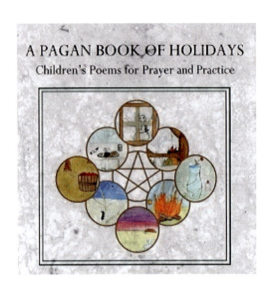

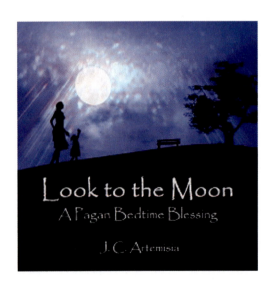

ABOUT THE AUTHOR

J.C. Artemisia is a communications professor with a master's degree in education and a bachelor's degree in creative writing. She is a pantheist Pagan and the proud mother to three, happy children. In addition to writing and visual art, she enjoys reading, crocheting, and baking up some kitchen magick. You can follow her updates and musings at www.facebook.com/JCArtemisiaBooks.

ABOUT THE ILLUSTRATOR

Sarah A. Chase is an artist and a writer. She homeschools her son, and she enjoys traveling and reading. Her writing and photography have been featured in magazines and on Elephant Journal. She lives in New England with her family. sarahachase.com.

Made in the USA
Monee, IL
04 December 2020